MARY MORRIS has been writing since
include several for young audiences.
theatre and for television. *Boss of the Pool* was Mary's first adaptation for the stage (from Robin Klein's novel). *Two Weeks with the Queen* was her second adaptation (from Morris Gleitzman's novel). Both toured nationally in Australia and *Two Weeks with the Queen* went on to tour as far afield as Canada, Cuba and the United Kingdom. *Blabbermouth* has toured nationally – including two seasons for the Melbourne Theatre Company.

MORRIS GLEITZMAN started his career as a screenwriter and by 1978 was the sole writer for three award-winning and top rating seasons of the *Norman Gunston Show*. His first two children's books, *The Other Facts of Life* and *Second Childhood* were followed by *Two Weeks with the Queen* which has received worldwide acclaim since its publication in 1990. His next novel, *Misery Guts*, received the 1992 Children's Book Council of Australia Honour Book award and was shortlisted for the NSW Premier's Awards. Subsequent publications include *Worry Warts*, *Blabbermouth*, *Sticky Beak* and, most recently, *Puppy Fat*. Gleitzman's work for TV and film includes *The Other Facts of Life*, which won a 1985 AWGIE award, *Harbour Beat* (1989) and *Second Childhood* (1990).

BLABBERMOUTH

The Play

MARY MORRIS

Adapted from the novel by
Morris Gleitzman

Currency Press • Sydney

CURRENCY TEENAGE DRAMA
General Editor: Katharine Brisbane
First published 1996 by
Currency Press Ltd,
PO Box 452, Paddington,
NSW 2021, Australia

10 9 8 7 6 5 4 3 2 1

Copyright © Mary Morris, Morris Gleitzman, 1996

This book is copyright. Apart from any fair dealing for the purpose of private study, research or review, as permitted under the Copyright Act, no part may be reproduced by any process without written permission. Inquiries concerning publication, translation or recording rights should be addressed to the publishers. Any performance or public reading of *Blabbermouth* is forbidden unless a licence has been received from the author or the author's agent. The purchase of this book in no way gives the purchaser the right to perform the play in public, whether by means of a staged production or a reading. All applications for public performance should be made to the author, c/o Hilary Linstead and Associates, Level 8, Plaza 11, 500 Oxford Street, Bondi Junction, NSW 2022

NATIONAL LIBRARY OF AUSTRALIA CIP DATA
Morris, Mary, 1944-
    Blabbermouth : the play
    ISBN 0 86819 421 2.
    1. College and school drama. 2. Mutism - Juvenile drama. 3. Physically handicapped - Juvenile drama. 4. Fathers and daughters - Juvenile drama. I. Gleitzman, Morris, 1953-. Blabbermouth. II. Title. III. Title: Blabbermouth. (Series : Teenage drama).
A822.3

Printed by Southwood Press, Marrickville, NSW
Cover design by Hana & Jana Hartig

Publication of this title was assisted by the Commonwealth Government through the Australia Council, its arts funding and advisory body.

Contents

BLABBERMOUTH

Act One   9
Act Two   47

Blabbermouth was first produced by the Melbourne Theatre Company at The Fairfax, VAC, 10 September 1993 with the following cast:

DAD	Michael Bishop
ROWENA BATTS	Doris Younane
DARRYN/MR COSGROVE/MR FOWLER/ AUCTIONEER/OFFICER/ANDY	Patrick Moffatt
MS DUNNING/YOBBO/MRS GRANGER	Merridy Eastman
AMANDA/YOBBO	Sally Cooper
MRS COSGROVE/MEGAN/YOBBO	Jane Turner

Directed by David Carlin
Designed by Trina Parker
Lighting by Greg Diamantis

A return season at the Melbourne Theatre Company at the Fairfax, VAC, opened 6 January 1995 with the following cast:

DAD/ANDY PECK/VOICES	Michael Bishop
ROWENA BATTS	Frances O'Connor
AMANDA	Jane Bayly
MS DUNNING/MRS GRANGER/TAMMY	Sue Giles
MR COSGROVE/MR FOWLER/DARRYN PECK	Francis Greenslade
MEGAN/MRS COSGROVE/OFFICER	Carole Patullo
MUSICIAN	Tom Lycos

Directed by David Carlin
Designed by Kim Carpenter
Music directed by Tom Lycos
Lighting by Jamie Revill-Henson

Characters

ROWENA BATTS
KENNY BATTS (DAD), Rowena's dad
AMANDA, Rowena's friend
MS DUNNING, Rowena's new teacher
TAMMY & MEGAN, school friends of Rowena and Amanda
DARRYN PECK, the class bully
MR & MRS COSGROVE, Amanda's parents
MRS GRANGER, Social secretary of the Progress Association
MR FOWLER, head teacher at Rowena's school
ANDY PECK, Darryn's brother

Setting

The present day. Various locations at home and school.

ACT ONE

SCENE ONE

ROWENA BATTS is on stage writing a letter as the opening song, 'Blabbermouth', is sung.

MUSICIAN My baby is the sweetest little thing
that I ever dreamed of
She came to me with ties of love
that wind around my heart
And when I look into her eyes
I know that's where my future lies
I swear that I will never
Ever ever let us part.
She's happy as the morning
that wakes up the little flowers
She's gentle as the sunbeams
that peek out between the rain
Sure as the moon is in the sky
I'll be with her until I die
'Cos when I'm with my baby
I don't ever feel no pain

ROWENA has finished the letter. She addresses the audience.

ROWENA This is going to be the best day of my life! A brand new school, the chance to make lots of friends and this [*She holds up the letter.*] is going to help me do it.

| MUSICIAN | Except that...
She's the biggest ever blabbermouth
Her lips reach right from north to south
Her voice is like the thunder
That makes rain fall from the skies
She's my blabber blabbermouth
Her lips reach right from north to south
But I'm a gonna love that gal until the day I die. |
|---|---|

SCENE TWO

ROWENA *has entered the classroom of her new school.*

MS DUNNING	OK. You can stop staring. I'd like to introduce you to our new class member. This is Rowena Batts. Well, say g'day.
ALL	Good morning Rowena.

ROWENA *signs good morning. They stare even more.* ROWENA *hands* MS DUNNING *the letter and points to the class.* MS DUNNING *reads it aloud.*

MS DUNNING	G'day. My name's Rowena Batts and I'm new to this school.
DARRYN	Miss! Miss!
MS DUNNING	Yes Darryn?
DARRYN	Miss, we already noticed that.
MS DUNNING	Mind your manners, Darryn Peck, or I'll kick you in the bum. [*She continues.*] The reason I'm writing this letter is I can't speak. The reason I can't speak is I was born with bits missing from my throat – It's OK but, I don't leak. [MS DUNNING *is the only one who laughs.*] Even

though I can't speak we can still be friends 'cause I can write, draw, point, nod, shake my head, screw up my nose and do sign language. Also I can hear. My hobbies are reading, watching tv and driving my dad's tractor. I hope we can be friends. Yours sincerely, Rowena Batts.

The class stare at ROWENA *like she's from outer space.*

MS DUNNING   Well. I think that was the best idea since microwave pizza. How'd you like to sit beside Megan, Rowena? [*She does.*] Who's on frogs? Darryn Peck?

DARRYN *swaggers to the frog's residence and picks up a small bucket.*

Clean it out properly this time, or I'll feed you to them.

DARRYN *gives* MS DUNNING *the finger behind her back. Everyone is too busy staring at* ROWENA *to laugh at him.*

Start reading the passage on page twenty-nine while I pop down to the office. I'll only be a sec. [*She exits.*]

DARRYN   I can speak sign language. [*He gives* ROWENA *the finger.*] What sort of a name is Batts? You fly around at night sucking people's blood?

ROWENA *does an imitation of a chook.*

She's a loony as well as a dummy.

MEGAN   No! She's a chook! Peck-peck-peck Get it? Darryn Peck!

DARRYN *picks up a frog and advances on* ROWENA.

DARRYN   How would you like to eat frog, dummy. Batts eat frogs, don't they?

ROWENA *mimes a chicken pulling something long and stretchy out of thc ground.*

MEGAN   Chickens eat worms!

BLABBERMOUTH

DARRYN	Her olds must really like having a kid like her around. Be as exciting as watching tv with the sound down. [*To* ROWENA.] Or are they freaks too and haven't noticed?
AMANDA	Leave her alone.
DARRYN	That's right, Cosgrove, you like freaks, don't you? Sorry, disabled persons. [*To* ROWENA.] What kind of freak's your dad? He a dummy too?
AMANDA	I said, leave her alone Darryn Peck!
DARRYN	And what about your mum. She a spazzo?

ROWENA *grabs the frog from* DARRYN*'s hand and stuffs it in his mouth. She grabs the bucket out of his other hand and rams it down over his head so he can't spit the frog out. The classroom empties.*

MUSICIAN	Oh yes she is the biggest ever blabbermouth
	Her lips reach right from north to south
	Her voice is like the thunder
	That makes rain fall from the skies
	She's my blabber blabbermouth
	Her lips reach right from north to south
	And I'm a gonna love that gal until the day I die.

SCENE THREE

MS DUNNING *speaks on the telephone. A cupboard is on stage.*

MS DUNNING	No, I wouldn't call it an emergency exactly. Perhaps if you could send a locksmith...
MR FOWLER	[*from off*] I'll sort this nonsense out, Ms Dunning, don't you worry about that!
MS DUNNING	[*to off*] It's alright, Mr Fowler, I'm getting a locksmith! [*to phone*.] No! Police Rescue won't be necessary...

MR FOWLER	Are you ringing the father? I asked you to ring the father.
MS DUNNING	I will.
MR FOWLER	Where is that blasted crowbar?!
MS DUNNING	[*to phone*] No, we don't need the fire brigade! It's just a kid locked herself in the stationery cupboard!
MR FOWLER	Ms Dunning!
MS DUNNING	[*yells*] What! [*To phone.*] Sorry.

MS DUNNING *exits. A lighting change allows the audience to see inside the cupboard.* ROWENA, *speaks to the audience.*

ROWENA	This is the worst day of my life. If they send for my dad, it'll be the end for me. Why did I do it? Why? Poor frog will probably get warts. He shouldn't have mentioned my mum. She died. One smart remark about her and I turn into Freddie Kruger and terrorise whole townships. How to ruin your life in two hours by Rowena Batts.

A state emergency OFFICER *enters carrying a huge axe.* MS DUNNING *and* MR FOWLER *follow.* MR FOWLER *carries a crowbar.*

OFFICER	She got any hostages in there?
MS DUNNING	No!
MR FOWLER	I thought you said a locksmith, Ms Dunning, not a lumberjack...
OFFICER	Have her out in no time.
MS DUNNING	I really don't think you ought to...
OFFICER	Tried talking her out, have we?
MS DUNNING	Yes, but...
OFFICER	To no avail?
MR FOWLER	Well obviously.
OFFICER	If you'll just step aside. Er... she's not armed, is she?
MS DUNNING	Of course not.

OFFICER	Kids today, slice you soon as look at you.
MS DUNNING	Look, I think we should try talking her out again.
MR FOWLER	This has gone too far, get out of my way.

MR FOWLER *takes to the cupboard with the crowbar, trying to prise it open. The crowbar slips and* MR FOWLER *skins his knuckles then drops the crowbar on his foot.*

	Damn! Blasted... bloody... blasted...
OFFICER	[*to audience*] Very nice! You can see where the kiddies get it from.
MR FOWLER	Rowena Batts! Come out of there at once!

MS DUNNING *picks up the crowbar.*

MS DUNNING	[*to cupboard*] Don't worry Rowena love, everything's going to be fine.

The roar of a truck engine is heard deep and throaty and full of hoon-power. Everyone freezes and listens as it gets louder and louder then subsides to a throbbing, growling idle, and stops.

Enter DAD *wearing cowboy boots, black jeans, studded belt with fancy buckle, loud satin shirt and a cowboy hat.*

DAD	G'day. Kenny Batts. [*Everyone is staring.*] This the cupboard?

MS DUNNING *nods.*

[*to cupboard*] You OK Tonto?

The door opens a crack and ROWENA*'s hands appear. She signs that she is ok.*

Tough day, huh?

Rowena's hands sign frantically, telling her story. DAD *watches.*

You were a chook? I don't get it. [*More signs.*] Oh, I get it, good one. [*More signs,* DAD *gets serious.*] He didn't.

[*More signs,* DAD *perks up.*] You didn't! [*More signs,* DAD *laughs.*].

MR FOWLER   We can't have a repeat of this sort of thing, Mr Batts.

DAD *is miming* DARRYN PECK *with his mouth full of frog.*

MS DUNNING   [*trying not to laugh*] It was just first day nerves, I'm sure it won't happen again, will it Rowena?

MR FOWLER   I fail to see the humour in the situation, Ms Dunning.

DAD   Now don't get your jocks in a twist. There's something you need to understand about me little mate here. Let me explain.

DAD *clears his throat loudly.* ROWENA *slams the cupboard door shut.* DAD *sings 'Heart Like A Fairground'.*

> When I saw my baby
> for the very first time
> I hoped I would hear her
> sweet voice say my name
> But I waited in vain
>
> 'Cos her lips are a graveyard
> Her teeth are tombstones
> my eyes are the rain clouds
> that fall from the sky
> and I'm soaked to the bone
>
> But her heart is a fairground
> she fills me with pride
> and I know she loves me
> 'cos I got free tickets
> for all of the rides.

When he is finished there is stunned silence. The door of the cupboard swings open and a very embarrassed ROWENA *is revealed.*

BLABBERMOUTH 17

DAD Now, ladies and gentlemen. Rowena Batts is taking the rest of the day off to go with her dad to the local milk bar and rot her teeth. If anyone's out of pocket for anything, give us a hoy and I'll bung you a bag of apples from the farm.

DAD *bends his knees, crosses his wrists and holds his hands out to* ROWENA. *She shakes her head at him – no, please. He nods firmly at her. She takes his hands, steps on his thigh and is swung onto his shoulders where she stands up straight.*

ROWENA [*to audience*] May as well face it Rowena. Your social life is finished.

DAD *and* ROWENA *exit.* DAD *singing a snatch of 'Walk Tall'.* MS DUNNING *stares after* DAD, *transfixed. She absently holds out the crowbar to* MR FOWLER *and drops it on his foot.*

SCENE FOUR

MR FOWLER *speaks to* ROWENA *slowly and loudly as if she's deaf.*

MR FOWLER Ah, Good morning Rowena. How are you today? Good, good. Um, a word with you before you go to class. I um, I know you've been used to a... special school and this move to a... normal school can't be easy for you, but, well to be blunt, Rowena, you're going to have to make a bit of extra effort to fit in – Yes? Now, I've spoken to Darryn Peck and Ms Dunning has told me your side of the story, but that doesn't excuse your disruptive behaviour. Understood? Good, Good.

AMANDA COSGROVE, *with* MEGAN, *enters and smiles shyly at* ROWENA.

Oh, and one more thing. Um, well, your father. I mean, if there are any problems... If you have a problem with him, say, drinking too much...

ROWENA *shakes her head, gets out a little notepad and starts to write.*

Yes, well, you do know you can talk to me about it. I pride myself on being a good listener. We also have a visiting school counsellor every second Thursday of the month...

She hands him the note, he reads aloud.

Dad hasn't let a drink pass his lips for years. Yes, um, good, good. Remember, Rowena, Ms Dunning's quite upset with you, so, special effort.

He exits. AMANDA COSGROVE *smiles again.* ROWENA *looks to see if* AMANDA *is smiling at someone behind her.*

AMANDA	Hello.
MEGAN	Hello.

ROWENA *signs hello.* MEGAN *giggles.* ROWENA *writes in her book, tears out the page and hands it to* MEGAN *who hands it quickly to* AMANDA.

AMANDA	[*after reading*] It's OK Rowena, the frog survived.
MEGAN	Darryn Peck sicked it up.

ROWENA *has written some more and hands it to* MEGAN *who passes it to* AMANDA.

AMANDA	[*reading*] My friends call me Ro.
MEGAN	What's wrong with you?
AMANDA	Megan!

ROWENA *writes and passes it to* MEGAN *who hands it straight to* AMANDA.

AMANDA	[*reading*] What's wrong with *you?*

MEGAN   Nothing!

ROWENA *takes all the pieces of paper from* AMANDA *and holds them pointedly in front of* MEGAN.

I'm just not very good at reading.

MS DUNNING *appears. She is frowning and pointing a gun at* ROWENA. AMANDA *and* MEGAN *throw themselves on the ground.* ROWENA *sticks her hands in the air.*

MS DUNNING   Oh, no, no! It's only the starter's pistol! Can't get the silly thing to work for the sports carnival tomorrow. Oh, by the way, Rowena, can you run? [ROWENA *nods.*] Thank goodness for that. I thought Amanda was going to have to run the girls' one hundred metres on her own. Can I put you down? [ROWENA *nods.*] Great!

MS DUNNING *suddenly acts super casual.*

Um... will your... um... father be able to come?

ROWENA *shakes her head. Definitely not.*

Oh. Pity.

MS DUNNING *wanders off fiddling with the pistol.*

MEGAN   You're mad!

ROWENA *writes and hands it to* MEGAN.

No. j,.. u... s... t... d... u... m... b... dumb!

MEGAN *giggles when she finally gets the joke.*

You are, but Amanda's the hundred metres champion of the whole school.

AMANDA   Megan!

ROWENA *mimes to* MEGAN *and* AMANDA *that she is a good runner too.*

Good one, we'll have a great race.

MEGAN You'll need all the help you can get, Ro. I hope your family are loud barrackers.

SCENE FIVE

Orchard. DAD, *wearing protective clothing, is spraying. He sings an old Mexican refrain – loudly.* ROWENA *enters and signs to him that he looks busy.*

DAD Yeh, looks like you won't be seeing much of me this weekend – It's a frontier out here, Amigo. Enemies all around us, a man can never rest. Weevils [*He blasts them.*] Mites, [*More blasts.*] Fungi, moulds, mildews! I'll jest round me up a posse and hunt them critters down. [ROWENA *nods.*] A man's gotta do what a man's gotta do, eh? Hope you didn't have anything planned.

ROWENA *signs happily. Nah, only her sports carnival, and that doesn't matter. She then gives the audience a surreptitious thumbs up sign, delighted that* DAD *can't come.*

Sports carnival! Tomorrow!?

Don't worry about it, signs ROWENA.

Aw, gotta be there Tonto.

ROWENA *desperately blasts at the 'critters', reminding him of the frontier.*

Nah, I wouldn't miss your sports carnival if a ten foot lump of blue mould jumped up and bit me in the goolies. Now, how'd you want to get there tomorrow? In the truck, or will we do it in style and take the tractor?

SCENE SIX

Sports carnival. MS DUNNING *talks through a megaphone.*

MS DUNNING Attention please. Would the people firing the starting pistol in the boy's toilets please return it immediately. That means you, Janice Holt! Now, the sack race. There's been a protest. Third place reckons second place had an unfair advantage 'cause her mum ironed the sack to cut down wind resistance! Only joking! Here are the results.

DAD *and* ROWENA *enter.*

Darryn Peck! Put down that javelin!
Um... Third place, Brian Jessop. Second place Kerrie O'Donnel. Equal first Guissepi and Guissepina Cassela. Silly twins, you were supposed to have a sack each! [*She sees* DAD *and forgets to lower the megaphone.*] Oh, Hello, Mr Batts.

DAD *winks at her. She drops all her race results. He helps pick them up.*

[*flustered, through the megaphone again*] Sorry... Thank you... um..I'll just... er... Darryn Peck!!!

She heads off after DARRYN PECK.

DAD I could have sworn my yellow and purple shirt was clean, and my black one with the red fringes. You sure you haven't seen them? [ROWENA *shakes her head, fingers crossed behind her back.*] And me new belt with the skeleton belt buckle! It was there, I laid it out on the bed this mornin' special! [AMANDA *waves to* ROWENA.] They look like a friendly mob. [ROWENA *signs that she's nervous about the race.*]. Tense huh? Well, you can't run a good race with your guts in a knot.

Come on, we'll relax you a bit.

DAD *'relaxes' her, beating her around the shoulders and back, and nearly shaking her arms out of their sockets.*

MR COSGROVE [*to* MRS CROSGROVE] Who are those... people?

AMANDA She's new at our school, her name's Rowena. She can't speak.

MR COSGROVE *seems interested.* ROWENA *staggers under* DAD*'s onslaught.*

DAD There, you're loosening up already. Breathe in. Hold. Breathe out! Come on, breathe in. Hold. Shame about me shirt. All those important people – parents, teachers and I can't even drum up a decent set of duds to make a good impression. Oh, sorry love, breathe out. Tell you what-

DAD *takes a horribly coloured kerchief from his pocket and ties it on cowboy style.* MR COSGROVE *tightens his own sober tie.*

– howsat? Good, let's mingle. [*He aims for the* COSGROVES.] G'day.

MRS COSGROVE Hello.

DAD Nice day for it.

MR COSGROVE Yes, very nice.

MRS COSGROVE Not too warm – for running, I mean.

DAD Yeh, beaut. The name's Kenny, anyway.

MRS COSGROVE How do you do Mr Anyway.

DAD No, no, Batts.

MRS COSGROVE Batts?

DAD Kenny Batts' me name, apple farming's me game.

MRS COSGROVE Oh! I see.

DAD And me sidekick, er, Rowena. [*To* ROWENA.] Say g'day

	Tonto. [ROWENA *signs g'day*.].
MR COSGROVE	Cosgrove. Douglas. My wife Mrs Cosgrove, my daughter, Amanda.

DAD *grabs* MR COSGROVE *by the hand and shakes it vigorously.*

DAD	Nice suit. Bet that cost a few bob. Criminal, the price of clothes these days.
MR COSGROVE	I own a menswear store.
DAD	Hey, you might be able to help me out. Last year at Tamworth Country and Western festival one of the singers was wearing this amazing pink satin shirt with a big black guitar on the back. I've tried writing to every mail order catalogue in the country for one like it. You wouldn't have one, would you?
MR COSGROVE	We don't stock satin shirts.
DAD	Y're mad mate. Big sellers satin shirts. I buy one at least every couple of months. [*To* ROWENA.] Don't I love?

DAD *becomes very interested in* MRS COSGROVE'*s bosom.*

MS DUNNING	Results of the one hundred metres boys. Third, Jason Johnson. Second, Martin Vimovich. First, Darryn Peck. How did that boy get so fast? Could it be because his brother Andy chases him to school every morning in his crop duster? Only joking! One hundred metres girls take your positions please.
DAD	[*still staring at* MRS COSGROVE'*s bosom*] Nobody move.
MRS COSGROVE	What? What is it?
DAD	Coddling moth. If you've got any apple or pear trees at home, these buggers'll go through 'em like guided missiles.
MRS COSGROVE	We haven't...
DAD	I have, but.

DAD makes several grabs for the moth and misses

Freeze! [MRS COSGROVE *does*.] I see where the sneaky beggar's gone.

DAD sticks his hand up the armhole of her dress. She screams.

Hold still, willya.

MR COSGROVE   Take your hands off my wife you... you maniac!
DAD   Ah! There it is. Stop wrigglin'. Got it!

DAD proudly shows everyone the squashed moth.

MR COSGROVE   You are a rude, unpleasant, badly dressed hoon!
DAD   Wha...
MR COSGROVE   Why don't you back off, go home and leave decent people in peace!
DAD   I was only trying to help, cheese-brain!

DAD turns to ROWENA and signs to her that the bloke's an idiot.

MR COSGROVE   What are you saying to her!? What's he saying!?
DAD   None of your business, pull your head in!
MS DUNNING   Girls one hundred metres to the starting line.
DAD   [*to* ROWENA] Get out there and show them your dust Tonto!

While DAD and MR COSGROVE eye each other off, AMANDA and ROWENA prepare to race.

ROWENA   [*to audience*] Cheese brain! I'm the cheese-brain for telling him about the stupid sports day in the first place. She was going to be my friend, now I'll be lucky if she ever speaks to me again!
MS DUNNING   Take your marks.
ROWENA   Deep breath, clear your head. If you can't have her for a friend, at least you can beat her in the race. Wait for it, wait for it.

MS DUNNING	Get set.
ROWENA	He called my dad a hoon!

The crack of a starting pistol. AMANDA *leaps ahead.*

	Concentrate! Got to catch her! [*She is catching* AMANDA.] Who needs friends anyway? More trouble than they're worth. Eat my dust Amanda Cosgrove! You with your pretty mum and your ordinary dad and your nice hair! [*She has passed* AMANDA.] Dad'll be so proud of me for winning. Oh, no, then he'll slap everyone on the back making them spill their drinks. [AMANDA *is catching up.*] He'll dig everyone in the ribs, making them drop their sandwiches! [ROWENA *sees* AMANDA *is level.*] Oh no you don't! I'd rather have my dad any day than a million friends. [ROWENA *surges forward again.*] But what if I win and he acts like such a hoon everyone here will rush home to get away from him. [AMANDA *is catching her again.*] We'll be the only ones left! Don't be a hoon, dad, don't be a hooooooooon!

AMANDA *and* ROWENA *cross the line together.* DAD *grabs* ROWENA *and swings her round.*

DAD	You beauty! You little beauty!
MR COSGROVE	Patently obvious Amanda crossed that line first. Congratulations Amanda.
MRS COSGROVE	I think its a draw, Douglas.
DAD	No way lady. Blind Freddie's dog could see Tonto here took the prize.
MR COSGROVE	My daughter won that race! You all saw her!

The COSGROVES *exit,* MR COSGROVE *pulling* AMANDA *off by the hand.* DAD *and* ROWENA *exit,* DAD *whooping and throwing her around in his joy.*

ROWENA	[*to audience*] This is the worst day of my life!

SCENE SEVEN.

School yard. ROWENA *slinks in*

ROWENA I'm invisible. [*To audience.*] Yes I am. Humiliation can make people invisible.

A kid enters. ROWENA *shuts her eyes. The kid looks at her, then runs off.* ROWENA *opens her eyes.*

See? Told you.

AMANDA *enters.* ROWENA *shuts her eyes tight.*

I'm invisible, I'm invisible.

AMANDA *stops in front of* ROWENA *and taps her. She opens one eye.* AMANDA *signs.*

[*to audience*] Huh?

AMANDA *signs slowly and painstakingly.*

[*to audience*] The flies *are* shocking today. [*She brushes away an imagined fly.*]

AMANDA *signs again.*

Nice turtle. Did she say nice turtle?

More signs.

Good air crash? I know! I'm suffering delayed sunstroke.

AMANDA *tries again.*

Good race. She's telling me I ran a good race. She's talking to me!

ROWENA, *signs back in a huge rush, asking her where she learned it.*

AMANDA Hey, slow down. I'm not that good – yet.

ROWENA *signs again slowly.*

> I learnt it last year. At a community service camp. I was scared to try it before in case you laughed at me.

ROWENA *signs at her to do more.*

> OK, Um...

She signs. ROWENA *reads the signs.*

ROWENA She doesn't like racing much, her parrot makes her do it. Mmm, how interesting.

ROWENA *makes the sign for parrot to* AMANDA. AMANDA *flaps her hands in frustration and tries again.*

> Oh, her father makes her do it.

More signs from AMANDA.

> Glue? [*She signs it again.*] Twin? [AMANDA *keeps signing.*] Friend. Friend! But what if I'm wrong!

ROWENA *signs to* AMANDA *to say it.*

AMANDA You want me to say it out loud?

ROWENA *nods and crosses her fingers.*

> Will you be my friend?

ROWENA *signs to* AMANDA, *inviting her home.*

> After school? [ROWENA *signs.*] Slow down! Yeh, that'll be great. As long as I can phone my Mum from your place and let her know I'll be late.

They exit. ROWENA *ducks back.*

ROWENA [*to audience*] This is the best day of my life!

SCENE EIGHT.

ROWENA's *place.*

AMANDA   I never seen so many apples! Does your dad own all those trees?

ROWENA *signs that she likes* AMANDA*'s hair.*

I reckon yours is nicer. Can I phone?

ROWENA *nods.* AMANDA *dials.* ROWENA *gets them both an apple.*

Hello? It's me. Mum, I'll be a bit late home I'm at a friend's house... Ro's place... Rowena Batts... No, he's not... [*Lowers her voice.*] Mu-um! Yes, I won't be very late... What for?... Oh, alright... Hello Dad. Yes, [*Lowers her voice more.*] He's at work. No I won't be long... No I haven't asked her yet... Yes, I will. Yes Dad... bye. [ROWENA *signs – is everything ok?*] Yeh, fine. He thinks you're really nice. [ROWENA *signs – what about* DAD.] No, they like him too, they do! Dad's really pleased we've made friends. Besides he's relieved I've finally got a community service project. [ROWENA *goes still.*] See, Dad's the president of the Progress Association and they're sponsoring a youth community service drive. That's where kids find someone who's disadvantaged and help them. Anyway, there's a community service night coming up and it's my turn to introduce a project to the other members. Dad thought I wouldn't get someone in time!

ROWENA *is backing away from* AMANDA.

I thought... I thought you could be my project. You could say no, if you like. Ro, say something. Please? [ROWENA *picks up an apple.*] Uh, I think I hear what you're saying...

ROWENA *lifts her arm.* AMANDA *runs for it.* ROWENA *throws the apple after her.*

ROWENA [*to audience*] I'm nobody's Community Service Project! If I wanted to be a project, I'd pin myself to the notice board in class. If I wanted to be a tragic case I'd go on '60 minutes' and look pathetic for the camera! If I wanted to be pointed at and sniggered at I'd cover myself in vegemite and chook feathers and dance in the shopping mall!

ROWENA *throws another apple.*

This is the worst day of my life!

She continues throwing. From off we hear DAD *yell 'ow!' He enters carrying all the thrown apples.*

DAD Hey, Tonto! That's no way to treat nature's bounty.

He juggles with the apples.

You look like you took a bite out of a big red shiny apple and found a worm inside.

ROWENA *makes him fumble, the apples hit the deck.*

Hmm, they're not much good for anything now, eh? Alright. What's the problem?

ROWENA *starts to tell him all about being betrayed by her new friend. He watches her hands solemnly.*

Jeez Tonto. Life's nuthin' but a bucket of blue mould.

DAD *sings 'Love Sucks' as* ROWENA *signs the lyrics. They dance,* ROWENA *standing on* DAD*'s feet.*

Love licks its lips and sucks you in
and chews you into pieces
It swallows you and chucks you up

and spits you out again.

Chorus.
Love sucks, love sucks, love sucks, love sucks,
It really really does, it really really does.
It really really does, it really really does.

Love breaks you up and tears you down
and rips your heart to fragments
demolishes your feelings
then it builds you up again.
Repeat chorus.
Love binds you up in ropes of pain
and chains you to the railings
It ties you up in little knots
then sets you free again.
Repeat chorus.

DAD Oh, I nearly forgot! This'll cheer you up.

DAD *takes a photo cutting from the paper out of his pocket and unfolds it.*

See, it's you and whatsername. This proves it – you're miles in front. [ROWENA *signs 'no way'.*] Weevil Poop! You're at least... two centimetres in front. [*She signs.*] It is not the angle of the camera!

ROWENA *holds the photo at arm's length trying to see if it is the angle of the camera.* DAD *notices an article on the back.*

Hey, look at this. Hold still [*He reads.*] Fund raising... Barbecue ... school oval... Sunday. Good one, I'll bung 'em a crate of apples to raffle. Um, you reckon that teacher – what was her name again – Will be there? [ROWENA *signs pointedly.*] Oh yeh, Ms Dunning.

[ROWENA *signs.*] She's mountain climbing in Venezuela on Sunday? – Pull the other one! [ROWENA *signs.*] What do you mean we can't go? [*She signs.*] So what if your ex-friend and her bozo dad are there? I won't start anything – unless he does. We'll just stick our noses in the air and be that dignified it'll make 'em spew. Oh, and this time I'm gonna make sure my purple and yellow satin shirt's clean.

He picks up the bruised apples.

Let's make some apple fritters for you to take to school tomorrow. Nothing makes friends faster than apple fritters, eh?

SCENE NINE

School yard. DARRYN, MEGAN, AMANDA *and* TAMMY *are hanging round.* ROWENA *takes a lunch box out, opens the lid and sniffs.* MEGAN *stops in her tracks.*

MEGAN What you got there?

ROWENA *holds up the lid of the box which has 'apple fritters' written on it.*

Nah, that's too hard, Let me see.

ROWENA *holds the lunch box out of sight and holds the words in front of her again. She stamps her foot, insisting that* MEGAN *try.*

A... p... p... l... e Apple. F... f... Fritt... frit-ters-fritters! Apple fritters!

MEGAN *is delighted with herself.* ROWENA *offers her one.*

I don't eat anything with apples in it, they give you cancer.

DARRYN: Frog fritters! Batts has got frog fritters.

AMANDA: Stop that, stop it!

ROWENA *starts to walk away.*

Wait!

AMANDA *walks up to her and takes a fritter. She bites it.*

DARRYN: Yuk! Amanda Cosgrove's eating a frog fritter!

AMANDA *takes a fritter and gives it to* MEGAN *and stares at her till she takes a bite out of it. Then she takes the box to* TAMMY *and wills her to take one.*

Don't eat them! You'll all get warts on your tongues from eating frogs.

AMANDA: You should know.

MEGAN: Warts nuthin! I'm gonna get cancer.

AMANDA: [*to* ROWENA] I'm sorry for expecting you to be my community project. I promise I'll never think of you that way again.

ROWENA *shrugs.* AMANDA *signs.* ROWENA *laughs.*

What are you laughing at? I just asked you to forgive me and be my friend. Is that so funny? [ROWENA *signs.*] I asked you to rub my elephant? Oh, sorry. But will you? Be friends?

ROWENA *doesn't reply.* AMANDA *takes her stillness as a no. She walks away.*

DARRYN: What's the matter, Cosgrove, you all upset? Aaw. I know how you feel — I'd be spewin' too if a spazzo beat me in the hundred metres.

MEGAN: They could both beat you any day Darryn Peck.

DARRYN: Oh yeh?

MEGAN   Yeh!

ROWENA *walks up to* DARRYN *and pokes him. She points to her chest and then to him.*

DARRYN   You and me? [ROWENA *nods.*] You reckon? [*She nods again.*] Go on then.

AMANDA   Leave her alone. I'll race you if it'll get rid of you.

ROWENA *stops her. She writes on her pad and gives it to* DARRYN *who reads it.*

DARRYN   The oval, Monday. Alright spazzo! You and me – Monday.

ROWENA *has been scribbling again.* DARRYN PECK *reads it. He looks at* ROWENA *and sneers.*

Perfect. You're on!

DARRYN *throws the paper down and stalks off.* MEGAN *picks it up, smooths it out and examines it as* ROWENA *signs to* AMANDA.

AMANDA   [*reading the signs*] OK... I will rub your elephant. Great!

MEGAN *finally deciphers the note.*

MEGAN   The... loser... has to ... eat a... frog!

The MUSICIAN *sings 'Leapin' Lizards'.*

MUSICIAN   Leapin' Lizards there's a frog in my soup
Lookin' at me sideways with its ole snake eyes
I don't think that I can get it down
Not unless it comes with shoe-string fries.

SCENE TEN

Darkness in the orchard. A torch moves about. DAD *is behind it, peering at trees, singing to himself.*

DAD: Her love was a beacon... my heart was a galleon... that smashed on the rocks and was lost...

MS DUNNING *creeps on. She taps* DAD. *He jumps.*

MS DUNNING: Sorry. It's me – Claire Dunning.

DAD: Jeez! Give a bloke a heart attack!

MS DUNNING: Sorry, there was nobody in the house so I thought you might be out here.

DAD: Tonto's not in strife at school, is she?

MS DUNNING: Oh, no! Um, what are you doing?

DAD: Checkin' for apple scab.

MS DUNNING: In the dark?

DAD: Got to keep on top of things. So what brings you out to a bloke's orchard of an evening?

MS DUNNING: Oh! I was... I mean... [*She bumps into a tree.*] Um... I was just... I wanted to ask you about a school project.

DAD: So how can I help you, teech? [*He looks into her eyes. She forgets what she's there for.*]

MS DUNNING: Um... Apples?

ROWENA *appears. She spies* MS DUNNING.

ROWENA: Shit! [*She hides.*]

MS DUNNING: I mean, fruit growing regions of Australia.

DAD: Oh.

ROWENA: [*to audience*] What's she doing here!? Oh God, I must be in the poo!

DAD: Hey look, the moon's coming out.

MS DUNNING	Yeh.
ROWENA	But I haven't had time to do anything really bad at school yet.
DAD	The orchard looks beaut in the moonlight.
MS DUNNING	Mmmm.
ROWENA	Maybe she's come to tell Dad I'm a child genius.
DAD	There's this fungus apple trees get – shines off 'em at night like little moonbeams – just beaut. I could show you?
MS DUNNING	That would be lovely.
ROWENA	But if I'm a child genius I'll have to go to a special school again! Just when I was making friends!

ROWENA *runs to stop* MS DUNNING *telling* DAD *to send her to a special school.*

MS DUNNING	G'day Ro.

ROWENA *signs frantically to* DAD, *asking what* MS DUNNING*'s doing here.*

DAD	Calm down Tonto. Teacher's not here to dob you in for anythin' – are you?
MS DUNNING	No. You can relax.
DAD	Course, if there's anythin' I ought to know, like if she's not behavin' herself, then I'll give her a goin' over for you. Like this!

DAD *demonstrates his version of giving* ROWENA *a going over by flipping her head over heels.* MS DUNNING *is highly amused.*

Howsat? You gonna behave at school?

ROWENA *signs at him 'what did you do that for?!'*

Goin' over. Get it? Well, I thought it was funny. Anyway Tonto, haven't you got homework to do?

ROWENA *shakes her head.*

Yes you have love.

ROWENA *shakes her head again.* DAD *signs to her that he wants to be alone with* MS DUNNING. ROWENA*'s chin hits the ground.*

MS DUNNING   What's he saying? What are you saying?

DAD   Ah, I was just saying to Ro, that since her and me usually go to the Copper Saddle for tea on Saturdays...

MS DUNNING   That's not what I've heard.

DAD   How do you mean?

MS DUNNING   I thought you went to town and beat her at pool and filled her up with hamburgers and milk-shakes on Saturdays.

DAD   Yeh, well we've decided to have a change and go somewhere flash this week. What I mean is, would you like to join us?

MS DUNNING   I'd love to.

DAD   Good. Now Tonto, Go and do your homework, [*Winks.*] while I take Ms Dunning down the path and demonstrate to her how to prevent fungus on apple trees.

ROWENA *signs, 'Oh yeh?'*

MS DUNNING   What did she say?

DAD   Oh, nothin'.

He winks broadly at ROWENA *again.*

MS DUNNING   Mmmm. I can see I'm going to have to learn sign language.

They exit.

ROWENA   The best teacher in the world wants to get on with my dad! I could be a bridesmaid!

'Here Comes The Bride' music plays. A bouquet lands in her hands.

Maybe she'll let me call her Mum! She'll make sure he wears white shirts and doesn't upset people and she'll make him keep his singing for the shower. Keeping my Dad in line will be a walkover for a woman who can make Darryn Peck spit his bubblegum into the bin!

SCENE ELEVEN

School yard. ROWENA *is in the school yard teaching* AMANDA *and* MEGAN *how to sign (something rude?).* MR COSGROVE *appears carrying some school t-shirts.*

MR COSGROVE	Amanda! Get off the ground! You're a young lady, not some drunken derro! [*He changes attitude when he sees* ROWENA.] Rowena! How are you? [ROWENA *signs, 'hello'.*] All ready for this evening?
AMANDA	Dad...
MR COSGROVE	We're very pleased you can come.
AMANDA	Dad there's been a ...
MR COSGROVE	You came along just in time you know. It would have been a rum do if the president's daughter had turned up at the community service evening without a project – eh?
AMANDA	Dad. You've got it wrong. Ro's not my community service project.
MR COSGROVE	But you told me she was. If she isn't who is?

MEGAN *snatches a book and starts 'reading' industriously.*

AMANDA	I haven't got one.
MR COSGROVE	I beg your pardon!?
AMANDA	I haven't got a community service project.

MR COSGROVE	But you said…
AMANDA	I'm sorry. I made a mistake.
MR COSGROVE	You mean you lied! Do you realise what you've done? You have let everyone down.
AMANDA	I didn't…
MR COSGROVE	That's enough! I hope you're ashamed of yourself. I'm ashamed of you, you know that? Deeply ashamed!

He stalks off. AMANDA *tries not to cry.*

MEGAN	Don't worry about him 'Mand. Hey, maybe if I pretend I can't read at all I could be your project.

AMANDA *shakes her head.*

SCENE TWELVE

Community service night. A woman (MRS GRANGER) *passes around a tray of nibbles and a bowl of dip to the audience. She approaches the* COSGROVES.

MRS GRANGER	It's going quite well, Don't you think?
MR COSGROVE	I'd like you to meet my wife, Mrs Cosgrove, and my daughter, Amanda. This is Mrs Granger, our new social secretary.
MRS GRANGER	Nice to meet you at last Amanda. I've heard so much about you from your father.

MR COSGROVE *looks at his speech, holding it at arm's length.*

MRS COSGROVE	Put your glasses on Douglas.
MR COSGROVE	I don't need glasses, it's the light in here.

MRS GRANGER *goes off to persuade people to try a nibble.*

	This is unforgivable, Amanda. How am I supposed to explain to all these people?

ROWENA *enters with* DAD.

MR COSGROVE: I've got a good mind to make you pick up that microphone and tell them what you've done.

MRS COSGROVE: Douglas, maybe you're being a bit...

MR COSGROVE: And maybe you don't realise the seriousness of the situation! I'm the President!

DAD: G'day Mr President.

MR COSGROVE: And to what do we owe the pleasure? Come to gloat?

DAD: [*to* ROWENA] Tell him, love. I couldn't trust meself not to spit in his eye!

ROWENA *signs.* AMANDA*'s face transforms.*

MR COSGROVE: What's she saying? Amanda! What's she saying?

DAD: She's saying, mate, that she's willing to put herself on the line for your daughter!

DAD *and* MR COSGROVE *lock eyes.*

AMANDA: Are you sure? [ROWENA *signs,* AMANDA *reads the signs.*] What are elephants for. Thanks Ro.

MR COSGROVE: Well, hadn't you better start introducing your er, Rowena around Amanda?

MRS GRANGER *approaches.*

MRS GRANGER: Would you like a nibble?

DAD: Ta. [*He takes a handful.*].

ROWENA *takes a couple of cocktail sausages.*

MRS GRANGER: Manners dear, what do you say?

ROWENA *sticks the sausages up her nostrils and signs, 'thank you'.*

AMANDA: Mrs Granger. This is Rowena Batts. She's vocally disadvantaged, but she's coping very well.

MRS GRANGER	Yes, well, nice to meet you dear. I must... duty calls.
AMANDA	Ro! Stop it. [ROWENA *signs.*] What do you mean you will if I will. What am I doing? [ROWENA *looks pathetic like for the '60 minutes' camera.*] OK I get it. Sorry.

ROWENA *takes the sausages out. Meanwhile,* MR COSGROVE *has taken the floor. He reads his speech with difficulty, squinting and holding it at arm's length.*

MR COSGROVE	Ah, distinguished guests, ladies and gentlemen, boys and girls. Welcome to the Progress Association's first Community Service night. Now, as you are aware, the purpose of these evenings is for our members to seek out, um, disadvantaged people in our community and give them a helping hand. And I can't stress enough how much it means to a less fortunate member of our society to have that hand put in front of them – the object being, to integrate these, um, people further into normal society so they can lead fuller, more rewarding lives and partake of the joys of, um, the joys. It is only fitting therefore, that the first person to demonstrate how helping her, um, hands have been, should be the daughter of my own self and my good wife. I'd like to call on Miss Amanda Cosgrove to introduce us to her, um. Thank you Amanda.

AMANDA *looks at* ROWENA *apologetically, then drags her in the spot.* DAD *whistles loudly.* COSGROVE *glares at him.*

AMANDA	Ladies and gentlemen, this is Rowena Batts and I'd like to tell you a bit about her.

ROWENA *taps her and signs.*

> Ah, Ro – Rowena says she'd like to tell you with her own helping hands. [ROWENA *signs with large movements.*] She says she'll leave it to you to work out whether she's vocally disadvantaged or an airport runway worker.

MR COSGROVE	What is she doing... wha... what... ?
MRS COSGROVE	It's a joke, Douglas.
AMANDA	She understands that some of you people here are disadvantaged.
MR COSGROVE	What did she say!?
MRS COSGROVE	Airport runway worker! [*She demonstrates.*]
AMANDA	She means you can't speak with your hands. And so she would like me to translate for you.

ROWENA *signs.*

MR COSGROVE	This is an outrage!
MRS COSGROVE	Shush Douglas, I want to hear her.
DAD	You heard your old lady, put a sock in it.
AMANDA	Ah, Ro says, 'I'm not a project, I'm a person. I've got problems making word sounds. Perhaps some of you have problems making a living, or a sponge cake. Or... Huh? [ROWENA *signs it again.*] Or number twos. You can feel sorry for me if you want. And I can feel sorry for you 'specially if number two's is your problem. But most of all I feel sorry for people who haven't got what I've got – a true friend.
MR COSGROVE	Friend! What she needs is a mother to teach her some manners!
DAD	Right! That's it!

DAD *grabs* MR COSGROVE. *They roll across the floor, locked in deadly combat.* MRS GRANGER *fails to get out of the way. The dip and the nibbles do exactly what is expected of them. The dads, after much ineffectual wrestling and slipping around in the mess, finally collapse exhausted and covered in food.*

ROWENA	[*to audience*] I wonder how old you have to be before you can run away and become a nun? No, it's a good idea. The other nuns have to be friends with you, no

	matter what your dad does. [*She kicks him in the leg.*]
DAD	I'm sorry Tonto, He mentioned your mum and I saw red. Hey, I'm still seein' red! [*He feels around his eyes and examines his fingers.*] God, the mongrel's bled me! [ROWENA *signs,* DAD *licks his fingers.*] Oh, you're right, it is beetroot juice.
MR COSGROVE	Hoon!
DAD	Ratbag mongrel!
MR COSGROVE	I'll have him arrested! Assault and battery!
DAD	[*to* ROWENA] Ooh, I've been stabbed. Right in the guts. [ROWENA *pulls his hands away from his middle in panic.*] No, no, its alright, it's me belt buckle. Aw cripes, he's bent me skeleton!
MR COSGROVE	Ought to be locked away!
MRS COSGROVE	Calm down Douglas, I'm sure I can get the stains out.
MR COSGROVE	Stains?! Stains?! I own a menswear store! Stains are not the problem! That... that... criminal is the problem! He's the one who can't control himself among decent people!
MRS COSGROVE	Ssssshhhh...
MR COSGROVE	And don't shush me! I won't be shushed, I'm the president!
DAD	I'll just go to the gents a minute love. [ROWENA *signs, anxious about him.*] Yeh, yeh, *I'm* alright, it's me best boots! I'll just have a go at wipin' the dip out of em before they're ruined. [*He squelches off.*]

MR COSGROVE *approaches* ROWENA.

MR COSGROVE	And as for you, young lady...
MRS COSGROVE	Now Douglas...

ROWENA *looks round for protection, but* DAD *'s gone.*

MR COSGROVE	Just you keep him away from me and my family.
AMANDA	Dad, don't...
MR COSGROVE	[*to* AMANDA] Be quiet! [*To* ROWENA.] I don't want him anywhere near me and I don't want you anywhere near my daughter. Keep away from her!
AMANDA	Mum, please...?
MR COSGROVE	Do you hear me?
MRS COSGROVE	Douglas...
MR COSGROVE	Do you!?

ROWENA *nods.* MR COSGROVE *grabs* AMANDA *by the hand to drag her away.* ROWENA *starts to sign. Nobody pays any attention. Finally* ROWENA *puts her fingers in her mouth and, to her surprise, a very loud whistle comes out.* MR COSGROVE *turns menacingly.* ROWENA *signs to him, slowly and bravely.*

Save it for those who are interested.

AMANDA *translates.*

AMANDA	You're not being fair.

MR COSGROVE *stops and glares at her.* AMANDA *continues to translate* ROWENA*'s signing.*

Just because you and Mr Batts can't be friends doesn't mean me and Ro can't be.

MRS COSGROVE	She's got a point, Douglas. It's like Israel and Palestine and Russia and America. Or Steve and Rob and Gail and Terry in *Neighbours*.
MR COSGROVE	Oh shut up! [*To* ROWENA.] Just you stay away from her.

MR COSGROVE *drags* AMANDA *off.*

MRS COSGROVE	Something has to be done about this!

She leaves.

ROWENA	She's right. I'm gonna have to tell Dad he's ruining my

life and if he doesn't pull his head in and apologise...

DAD *returns in his socks, sadly regarding his ruined boots in his hands.*

Well, here goes nothin'.

DAD *looks at her dismally as she signs, 'what a fine mess he's made of things.'*

DAD You're dead right Tonto, it is a flamin' disaster. [*She signs again.*] Yep. I'm gonna have to do something drastic to save the situation. [*She signs, 'he better do it fast.'*] Yeh, but... [*He examines the boots.*] It could make things worse, though. [*She signs, 'no it won't.'*] Okay. It's worth a try. Yeh. I'm gonna do it – eh? [*She nods happily.*] I'm gonna do it now, I'm gonna go home and put the hose in me boots!

END OF ACT ONE

ACT TWO

SCENE THIRTEEN

At The Copper Saddle. ROWENA, MS DUNNING *and* DAD *are seated by a frilly-shirted* WAITER *and handed huge menus.*

DAD Down to business, eh? Now what'll I have...

ROWENA *holds the menu up to hide her face from* DAD *and* MS DUNNING.

ROWENA Please don't ask for a plate of dead cow, please don't ask for a plate of dead cow, please don't ask for...

DAD A plate of... steak please mate.

ROWENA Phew.

DAD Pretty fancy tucker – eh? [*To* WAITER.] Hey, nice shirt mate.

This WAITER *is used to classier joints and white shirts.*

Be better in red though. [*To* MS DUNNING.] What're you having?

MS DUNNING The frogs legs sound nice, don't they Ro? Only joking! I'll have the chilli octopus.

DAD What'll you have Tonto?

ROWENA *points to something on the menu.*

Ah, she'll have...

The WAITER *holds up a hand to shush* DAD.

WAITER [*to* ROWENA] Madam has hearing? Lip reading? [ROWENA *points to her ear and nods.*] Then may I take your order please? [*She signs.*] Chicken in filo pastry? Certainly Madam.

He stalks off full of upmanship.

DAD   Woah, classy joint eh?

ROWENA *signs to* DAD *to tell* MS DUNNING *something.*

I'm not tellin' her that!

ROWENA *signs to* MS DUNNING.

[*to* ROWENA] Give a bloke a break.

MS DUNNING   [*to* DAD] Go on, tell me.

DAD   She says I'm good at fixin' things. Jeez, Tonto.

MS DUNNING   And are you? [ROWENA *nods emphatically that he is.*] Good.

ROWENA *signs that* DAD *'s sexy looking.*

DAD   Aw, cut it out!

MS DUNNING   What did she say?

DAD   There's some things a bloke can't say about himself.

MS DUNNING *catches on.* DAD *doesn't know where to put himself.*

Change the subject eh?

MS DUNNING   OK. You two are coming to the Parents' and Teachers' Barbecue tomorrow aren't you? It should be a good day. We've got a raffle. And an auction.

DAD   Auction?

MS DUNNING   Just stuff people donated.

DAD   I might donate something m'self.

MS DUNNING   You got something worth bidding for?

DAD   Could be.

They look in each other's eyes. They forget all about ROWENA. *She gives the audience a big thumbs up.*

ROWENA   Now all I got to do is make her realise the advantages of having a daughter who's already been breast fed and who never talks back and my troubles are over!

The meals arrive. They are huge.

DAD   Cripes mate, this'll put meat on our bones.

MS DUNNING   [*to* WAITER] Thank you. [*To* DAD.] We're having lots of other events. Um, Chicken kebabs for the barbie – a sky-writing display.

DAD   Sky writing? Straight up?

MS DUNNING   Darryn Peck's big brother Andy in his crop duster.

The WAITER *pours wine in* MS DUNNING*'s glass.* DAD *puts his hand over his.*

Would you rather have a beer?

DAD   Nah. I don't drink.

MS DUNNING   Oh, really?

DAD   Yeh, got into it a bit too heavy for a while – after Je... Ro's mum died. Bad news, wasn't it, Tonto? [*She agrees.*] Had to give it away.

MS DUNNING   Right.

DAD   See, one day I took off uphill after me usual liquid lunch without securin' the tailgate of the truck. Lost me load. [ROWENA *joins in the story, madly signing.*] Yeh, like she says- seventy cases of Granny Smiths rolling down the main street at rush hour. Phew! Talk about apple puree. Jeez, I had a reminder for weeks not to touch a drink again.

ROWENA *signs to be excused.*

Oh, right, [*To* WAITER.] Where's the dunny mate?

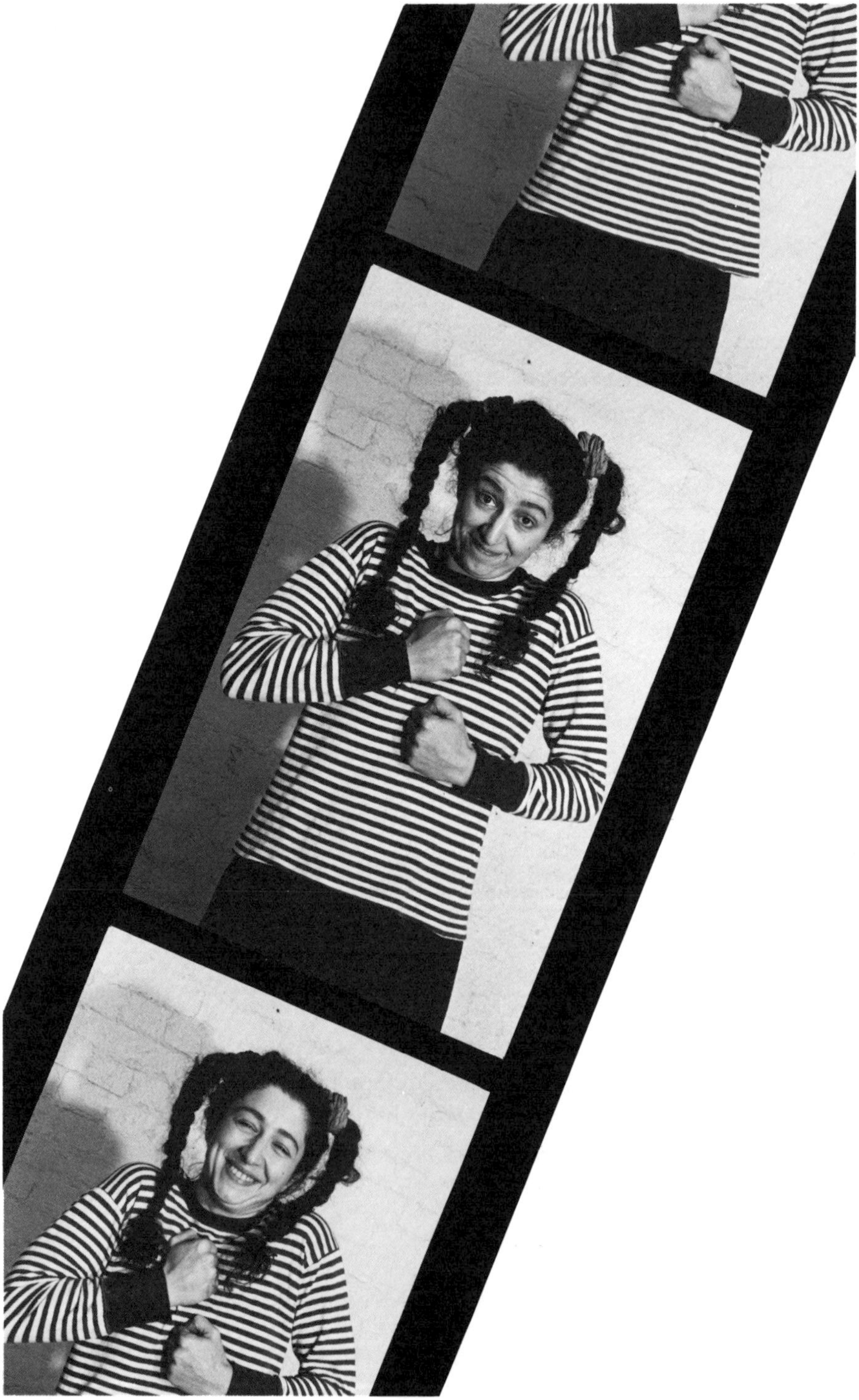

ROWENA *kicks him under the table. The* WAITER *points off discreetly.* ROWENA *starts to exit.*

DAD Oh, and lift the seat up love.

The WAITER *stops in his tracks and looks at* ROWENA, *then at* DAD – *but she's a girl?*

Redbacks. Don't want her to get her bum bitten – eh?

ROWENA [*as she exits*] I'm invisible, I'm invisible...

MS DUNNING I think she's a bit embarrassed.

DAD Nah, she's right.

MS DUNNING You do tease her a bit.

DAD Keeps her tough – which I reckon isn't a bad thing for a kid like her.

MS DUNNING I don't think I can eat all this.

DAD Yeh, bit of a challenge. Tell you what, let's shuffle the grub down a bit, make some more room.

DAD *bounces up and down on his chair.*

Come on, we don't want to waste it.

MS DUNNING *joins in, laughing. It gives her hiccups.*

Hey, I know what you do for hiccups. What you do is drink some water from the wrong side of the glass.

MS DUNNING *tries and fails, they laugh as she dribbles it.*

MS DUNNING It's impossible!

DAD Nah, you can do it.

DAD *tries. He dribbles too. He gets determined and gets into some acrobatic contortions trying. He spills the water.* ROWENA *returns in time to see it.*

ROWENA Oh no! She must be so embarrassed. She'll never want to go out with him again. I never want to go out with him again!

DAD *starts to do a hand-stand on the chair so he can come at the glass upside down.*

ROWENA Am I gonna have to write it in letters fifty foot high before he understands?!

ROWENA *puts her fingers in her mouth and whistles loudly. The* WAITER *drops a platter.* DAD *stops.*

Whoah Tonto! Where'd you learn that?

ROWENA *signs that she would like to go home.*

DAD You want to go home? Why?

ROWENA *signs that she is not feeling well.*

[*to* MS DUNNING] She's feelin' crook. What's the matter, is it your guts?

ROWENA *pretends it's a headache.*

MS DUNNING Let's get you home to bed.

They start to leave. ROWENA *stops and signs 'sorry' to the* WAITER.

WAITER Not a problem, Madam, we have plenty more in the kitchen. [ROWENA *signs.*] You're very welcome, Madam.

They exit. The WAITER *wheels off the mess.*

And she thinks she's got a headache!

SCENE FOURTEEN

ROWENA *knocks on the* PECK*'s door. The door opens letting out a blast of head-banging music.* DARRYN *appears. He has to shout to be heard. The whole scene is conducted in loud and aggressive yelling.*

DARRYN What do you want, spazzo?

ROWENA *signs something to the effect that he'll be eating frog again if he's not careful. Of course* DARRYN *hasn't got a clue what she's signing.*

DARRYN Get lost!

He starts to shut the door. ROWENA *thrusts a note at him. He looks at it.*

VOICE [*from within*] Who is it!
DARRYN She wants Andy!
VOICE Andy!
ANDY [*from within*] What?!
DARRYN She wants ya to do a job in the plane!
ANDY Tell her to get lost!
DARRYN Get lost!

DARRYN *goes to shut the door.* ROWENA *holds up a wad of money.*

She's got cash!

The loud music stops instantly on that magic word. There is a pause while DARRYN *stands curling his lip at* ROWENA *who still holds her money up. Suddenly* DARRYN *flies out the door propelled by a hand that has appeared from the dark recesses of the doorway. The hand wraps itself round* ROWENA*'s t-shirt front. She trembles and looks at the audience for help. Suddenly she disappears – yanked inside, money and all.* DARRYN *tries to follow. The door slams in his face. He slinks off stage.*

SCENE FIFTEEN

School Barbecue.

MR FOWLER And now ladies and gentlemen, boys and girls, we come to the last item of our auction. But before I offer it to you, might I say I am more than gratified by your generous response to all the items that heretofore fell under my hammer so to speak. My willing helpers with the money jar tell me the proceeds so far have exceeded our expectations to the tune of half a new carpet for the library. Well done one and all.

DAD *and* MS DUNNING *hop on in sacks laughing and elbowing each other, both trying to win.* ROWENA *hops behind.*

MR FOWLER	Now, What am I offered for this beautiful ornamental um... vase?
DAD	Jeez, Look at that!
MR FOWLER	Fifty cents?
DAD	Nice eh? Five bucks!
MR FOWLER	Sold!

DAD *collects the vase and presents it to* MS DUNNING. ROWENA *is searching the sky anxiously.*

That concludes today's auction — unless there are any late entries?

DAD *approaches* MR FOWLER *and whispers in his ear.*

Er, well thank you, but we wouldn't want to put you to all that trouble.

DAD	Nah, it's alright. Give us a bit of a build up eh?
MR FOWLER	Er, Yes. Good. Ladies and gentlemen, Mr Batts has offered to give us a rendition in his own voice of a ballad in the country and western style of musicianship.
ROWENA	Oh no! Where are you Andy Peck?!

DAD *whispers the story to* MR FOWLER.

MR FOWLER It tells the touching story of a yodelling cowgirl who gets... um... [DAD *whispers.*] gets laryngitis and can't warn her lover on the other mountain of an

		impending avalanche.
ROWENA		If he's flown off to Western Australia with my life savings I'll hunt him down if it takes the rest of my life.
MR FOWLER		What am I bid for Mister Batts? You madam is that a bid? I see, you're just sticking your fingers in your ears. Come on, ladies and gentlemen. Who will give me a dollar for Mr Batts to er... sing.
MS DUNNING		Ten dollars!
MR FOWLER		A handsome bid, Ms Dunning. Are there any more bids? Ten dollars once... ten dollars twice for Mr Batts to sing...
MS DUNNING		No, the ten dollars is for him not to sing.
MR FOWLER		Sold!

MS DUNNING *hands over the money.* MR FOWLER *leaves.* AMANDA *enters and approaches* ROWENA.

AMANDA Hi Ro!

ROWENA *looks around for* MR COSGROVE *and signs to* AMANDA *that she's not allowed to talk.* DAD *also looks for* COSGROVE.

[*to* ROWENA] It's alright, Dad's parking the car. I can't talk long, but. Ro, I'm really sorry about all this. [ROWENA *signs: 'me too'.*].

DAD G'day Amanda.

AMANDA Hello Mr Batts.

DAD [*moving protectively to* ROWENA] You right there Tonto?

ROWENA *signs to* DAD *that she's ok, she wants to talk privately to* AMANDA.

Alright, love – I'm just over here, right?

AMANDA Mum says Dad'll calm down. And we can still be friends at school, can't we? [ROWENA *nods, they chat in sign language.*].

MR COSGROVE enters.

MR COSGROVE Amanda! Stop that at once.

DAD hears him.

AMANDA I was just saying hello.

MR COSGROVE I won't have you doing this secret society stuff.

DAD advances on MR COSGROVE.

AMANDA It's just sign language Dad...

MR COSGROVE You are not a handicapped person! You have a perfectly good voice.

DAD Look mate...

MR COSGROVE And I thought I made it perfectly clear that you are to keep away from these... People!

DAD That's it! I've had enough.

ROWENA Save me, Andy Peck, save me!

DAD It's time someone gave you a short sharp message, and I'm the one who's gonna do it!

MR COSGROVE Oh, and what message is that then?

DAD You're just about to find out, mate!

We hear the faint drone of a plane engine. The two men eyeball each other.

MEGAN Look! The sky writing!

MS DUNNING Come on, you two. Don't spoil everything.

ROWENA [*to audience*] Yes!

DAD You'll keep, mate.

MR COSGROVE You all heard him threaten me!

The plane noise gets louder.

AMANDA Look, there he is!

MS DUNNING He's writing!

MR COSGROVE	I can't make it out. Is that a D?
MS DUNNING	No, it's an F.
AMANDA	I think it's an R
MEGAN	What's the matter with you? Can't you read? It's a P!

All look at her in surprise as she points at each letter.

	P... U... L... L.
MR COSGROVE	Put your best foot forward!
ROWENA	[*to audience*] It's working, he's doing it!
MS DUNNING	That's not the school motto!
MEGAN	There's more, let me, let me! Y... O... U... R.

All the heads follow the writing in unison as it unfolds.

MS DUNNING	The school motto is 'Forward, not Back.'
MR COSGROVE	Yes, I can see it now, plain as day. 'Forward, not Back.'
AMANDA	Put your glasses on Dad!
MEGAN	H... E... A... D... I... N... Pull your head in!
ALL	Pull your head in?
AMANDA	There's more.
ROWENA	This is it. The end of all our problems. I *am* a child genius!
MEGAN	D... A.... D. Dad! Pull your head in Dad!
AMANDA	Pull your head in Dad... ?

DAD *starts to laugh.*

DAD	Gor, that's priceless!
ROWENA	I knew he'd take it well.
DAD	Here's me gettin' on my high horse gonna tell cheese-brain here to pull his head in and she thinks up a way of doin' it that beats all! Jeez Amanda, you'll go far!
AMANDA	It wasn't me...

DAD	[*to* MR COSGROVE] You hear what your daughter's trying to tell you mate? Can she make it any clearer than that? eh?
AMANDA	I didn't do it.
DAD	What, was it your Mum?
AMANDA	It wasn't anybody in my family.
DAD	Well who was it then?

A shocked silence. Everyone is looking at ROWENA. DAD *goes quiet.*

MEGAN	I'm outta here! [*She goes.*]

ROWENA *looks at* AMANDA. AMANDA *looks at her a long time.*

MR COSGROVE	Yes, Well. We'll be off then. [*They exit.*]
MS DUNNING	I'll see you at school Rowena.

MS DUNNING *touches* DAD*'s arm gently then leaves.* DAD *continues to look at* ROWENA.

DAD	You did that for me?

She nods. DAD *turns and walks away.*

ROWENA	[*to audience*] He's just bluffing. He'll wait in the truck for me, face like a full tick and when I get in he'll kill himself laughing. He'll tickle me and ruffle my hair and say I'm a real case and he's going to mind his manners from now on.

The sound of a truck starting and taking off. ROWENA *runs off.*

SCENE SIXTEEN

At home, ROWENA *runs in looking for* DAD. *She whistles loudly, he doesn't appear. She finds money and a note. She reads it.*

ROWENA	Dear Rowena. I feel pretty crook about all this and I

can't think straight right now so I'm taking a hike. Go and stay with Amanda. Dad.

ROWENA *sees an empty bourbon bottle lying on the floor. She picks it up. She starts to cry. She picks up the phone and punches a number.* AMANDA *enters holding a mobile phone.*

AMANDA Hello? [*There is no reply.*] Hello. Hello-o. Who is this? [ROWENA *tries to whistle, tears stop her.*] Is this some kind of sick joke? [ROWENA *keeps trying.*] Is that you Darryn Peck? Whoever you are I'm hanging up now and I'm going to phone the police!

AMANDA *hangs up. She is just about to stalk off but stops in her tracks. She thinks, then punches a number.* ROWENA'S *phone rings. She looks at it a long time – what's the use?*

Come on, answer! [ROWENA *picks it up.*] Hello? [*silence*] Ro, is that you? [*Silence.*] Did you just phone me? [ROWENA *nods helplessly.*] If it was you, make a noise for me. [ROWENA *bangs the bottle.*] OK, good. Are you alright? [*Silence.*] If you're alright make one noise. If you're not, make two. [ROWENA *makes two.*] Ro, I'm going to hang up now and get Dad and we're coming to get you. OK? [ROWENA *bangs once.*] OK. Hang on Ro, Hang on.

SCENE SEVENTEEN

MR *and* MRS COSGROVE *wheel in a camp bed and make it up while* ROWENA *and* AMANDA *fetch* ROWENA*'s gear from the car.*

MR COSGROVE Sergeant Vinelli says there's not much they can do tonight.

MRS COSGROVE It's not like he's a missing person, he went of his own volition.

MR COSGROVE	How dare he leave her a note to tell her to live with us!
MRS COSGROVE	She's a child in need....
MR COSGROVE	That's not the point! It's the cheek of the man.
MRS COSGROVE	She's got nobody.
MR COSGROVE	Better off if you ask me.

ROWENA *and* AMANDA *enter with some of* ROWENA's *gear.*

	I'll contact child welfare in the morning.
MRS COSGROVE	[*loudly, to warn* MR COSGROVE *of* ROWENA's *presence*] Ahem! Yes it is lovely to have a special little guest, isn't it Amanda?
MR COSGROVE	Pleased to have you. Hope you'll be comfortable.
MRS COSGROVE	Only a rickety old camp bed, I'm afraid!
AMANDA	[*reading* ROWENA's *signs*] She says, 'thank you'. She's very grateful.
MRS COSGROVE	No need love, you're very welcome.
AMANDA	You can stay here forever. Can't she?
MR COSGROVE	Yes, well, um, any more things to bring in?

AMANDA *and* ROWENA *leave.*

	I don't like Amanda getting too... attached.
MRS COSGROVE	Now, what's wrong with being attached? I can think of worse people for Amanda to be friends with.
MR COSGROVE	I hope they catch that hoon and throw him in jail.
MRS COSGROVE	The school will have to be informed. Maybe she should have a day or two off.
MR COSGROVE	No, best if she gets right back in there.
MRS COSGROVE	Maybe the community service committee can help out in some way.
MR COSGROVE	A fund! A special fund to help tragic cases like this.

The tragic case enters staggering under a case of apples. She dumps it in MRS COSGROVE's *arms.* AMANDA *follows with the last of the gear.*

MRS COSGROVE: We have plenty food, dear. [ROWENA *signs.*]
AMANDA: Ro says she wants to contribute something.
MR COSGROVE: Good attitude. Well done.
MRS COSGROVE: Yes, well these'll, um, yes...
MR COSGROVE: Maybe you can help out in the shop after school eh? [ROWENA *nods.*].
MRS COSGROVE: Have you any more things? [ROWENA *shakes her head.*] Well. I'll put these in the kitchen. They'll last us a while, I'm sure.

ROWENA *brings out a battered recipe book from her luggage. And holds it in front of* MRS COSGROVE's *face.*

A hundred and one things to do with apples. [ROWENA *dumps the book on top of the apples.*] Lovely. Thank you.

MR COSGROVE: Amanda, it's already past your bed-time.

MR *and* MRS COSGROVE *exit.*

AMANDA: I wish you could be in my room. [ROWENA *signs: 'me too'.*] Dad didn't think it was a good idea. Maybe he thought you'd keep me awake all night with your noisy chatter. Will you be alright? [ROWENA *nods.*] Sure? [*Nod.*]

MRS COSGROVE *comes back from the kitchen.*

MRS COSGROVE: [*to* AMANDA] Come on dear, it's late.
MR COSGROVE: [*also back*] Off with you now.
AMANDA: Goodnight Ro. 'Night Mum. 'Night Dad.

ROWENA *watches as* MR *and* MRS COSGROVE *hug and kiss* AMANDA *tenderly.*

MR COSGROVE   Well, ah, sleep well Rowena.

MRS COSGROVE   See you in the morning dear.

They exit, the picture of a happy family.

ROWENA   The human organism can survive any amount of sadness — if it keeps busy.

ROWENA *tries to be busy. She opens her suitcase and starts to unpack. She unpacks an old teddy. She also unpacks a sandwich. She takes a bite out of it and puts the rest under her pillow.*

The MUSICIAN *sings, 'Someone To Turn To'.*

MUSICIAN
>When I was a baby
>and felt insecure
>I'd reach for my teddy
>To help see me through.
>
>Soft toys of my childhood
>they kept me from harm
>my favourite blanket
>all tattered and worn
>All loved and familiar
>to cuddle and hold
>when I was a youngster
>they kept out the cold

ROWENA   [*still unpacking*] Oh no! I forgot my jammies!

She gets into bed in her undies, hugging the teddy.

Everything's going to be fine. OK, so I'm a charity case. That's alright. Maybe they'll send me to a special school again. At least there'll be people there who understand me now that he's g... g... g... not here. It's a relief really. I mean, all my life, as long as I can remember I've been scared deep down that he would leave me. Well, now I

MUSICIAN
    don't have that worry any more, do I?
    But now that I'm older
    and things get too rough
    I find those old comforts
    no longer enough

AMANDA *enters, she sings the next few lines.*

AMANDA
    I need someone to lean on
    the touch of a hand
    a shoulder to cry on
    a smile from the heart

AMANDA *is now sitting in bed with* ROWENA. *She,* ROWENA *and the* MUSICIAN *harmonise the rest of the song.*

ALL
    Will you be that someone
    my own special friend
    my someone to turn to
    on side till the end

Chorus.

    someone to turn to
    someone to turn to...

AMANDA *and* ROWENA *snuggle down,* AMANDA *puts her arm around* ROWENA. *The* MUSICIAN *fades out the song.*

SCENE EIGHTEEN

School yard. AMANDA, MEGAN *and* ROWENA *enter.* TAMMY *stares at* ROWENA. DARRYN *has his lunch-box.*

AMANDA   What are you staring at?
TAMMY   Nothing.
MEGAN   Anybody'd think you'd never seen an abandoned kid

before.

DARRYN Ready for the race Batty? Hope you didn't bring any lunch, 'cos I got it right here!

ROWENA *had forgotten the race.* MEGAN *examines the contents of the lunch box.*

MEGAN Yuk, Darryn Peck, you didn't have to bring a boy frog – it's huge!

AMANDA She doesn't feel like running today.

DARRYN She's chickening out! [*He makes chicken noises.*].

AMANDA She's not! She just doesn't feel well today. I'll race you Darryn peck-peck chicken!

DARRYN Loser eats this. [*The frog.*]

AMANDA I know.

ROWENA *advances on* DARRYN. *She makes the sign for tomorrow.*

She says she'll race tomorrow.

DARRYN The deal was to race today. You're the loser, Batts. I hope you've got a good appetite.

AMANDA Are you deaf Darryn Peck! She says she'll race you tomorrow and unless you want me to ram that frog down your throat myself, you better agree. Right!?

DARRYN Phaw. You and who's army?

MEGAN *lines herself up with* AMANDA. ROWENA *adds her body to the line-up.* DARRYN *suddenly sees sense.*

Tomorrow, Batts, Or the whole school gets to know you're a yellow chicken.

MEGAN And we'll look after the frog tonight so we can feed it lots and lots of flies. We want it nice and fat so you choke on it!

MS DUNNING *approaches as* DARRYN *leaves.*

MS DUNNING	Hi Rowena, You OK? [ROWENA *nods.*] Heard anything? [ROWENA *shakes her head.*] By the way, What was all that stuff with Darryn Peck?
MEGAN	Oh, It's just a little race Ro and Darryn are having. Just for fun.
MS DUNNING	Fun, eh? And what about the frog?

Big guilty silence.

MEGAN	Ah, Um, That's what they're racing for.
MS DUNNING	I can think of more attractive prizes. [*She exits.*]

ROWENA *signs at* MEGAN.

MEGAN	What she say?
AMANDA	She reckons you're a future prime minister!
MEGAN	[*growing visibly*] Yeh!

SCENE NINETEEN

Amanda's house. A cloud of smoke surrounds ROWENA *who is sobbing over a plate of apple fritters.* MRS COSGROVE, *screaming, runs on with a chip pan,* AMANDA, *screaming, flaps a dish towel at the smoke.* MR COSGROVE, *yelling, runs around with a fire extinguisher.*

MR COSGROVE	What is going on here! Explain yourself young lady!

ROWENA *signs.*

AMANDA	She was making apple fritters.
MR COSGROVE	Apple fritters! It's six-o-clock in the morning! [ROWENA *is still signing and sobbing.*]
AMANDA	She always makes apple fritters when she's depressed.
MR COSGROVE	At six in the morning! Everyone's depressed at six in the morning!

MRS COSGROVE	Douglas, there's no harm done.
MR COSGROVE	No harm done?! No harm done!!!!
AMANDA	She says they were for your breakfast.
MR COSGROVE	Breakfast! We were nearly burned in our beds and you talk to me about breakfast!
MRS COSGROVE	Douglas...
MR COSGROVE	I won't have it! You hear? I won't...
MRS COSGROVE	DOUGLAS!!!! [*He looks at her.*] I said, there's no real harm done. It was a nice thought, Rowena. Thank you. [*She takes the plate from* ROWENA.]
MR COSGROVE	Have you gone mad? The house nearly burned down round our ears and all you can say is thank you! You all heard her, she's gone mad!
MRS COSGROVE	[*quietly*] Douglas.

He stops. She rams an apple fritter in his mouth and exits.

SCENE TWENTY

DARRYN PECK *is stretching and warming up.* MS DUNNING *enters.*

MS DUNNING	Well, Darryn. Warming up for the race?
DARRYN	Uh. Yeh, Miss.
MS DUNNING	I just wanted to tell you how pleased I am that you're doing so much to help Rowena Batts settle in.
DARRYN	Me, Miss?
MS DUNNING	Inviting her to games on the oval.
DARRYN	Oh. Yeh, Miss.
MS DUNNING	She's going through a bad patch just now and I appreciate how you are making a special effort to get her to join in things.

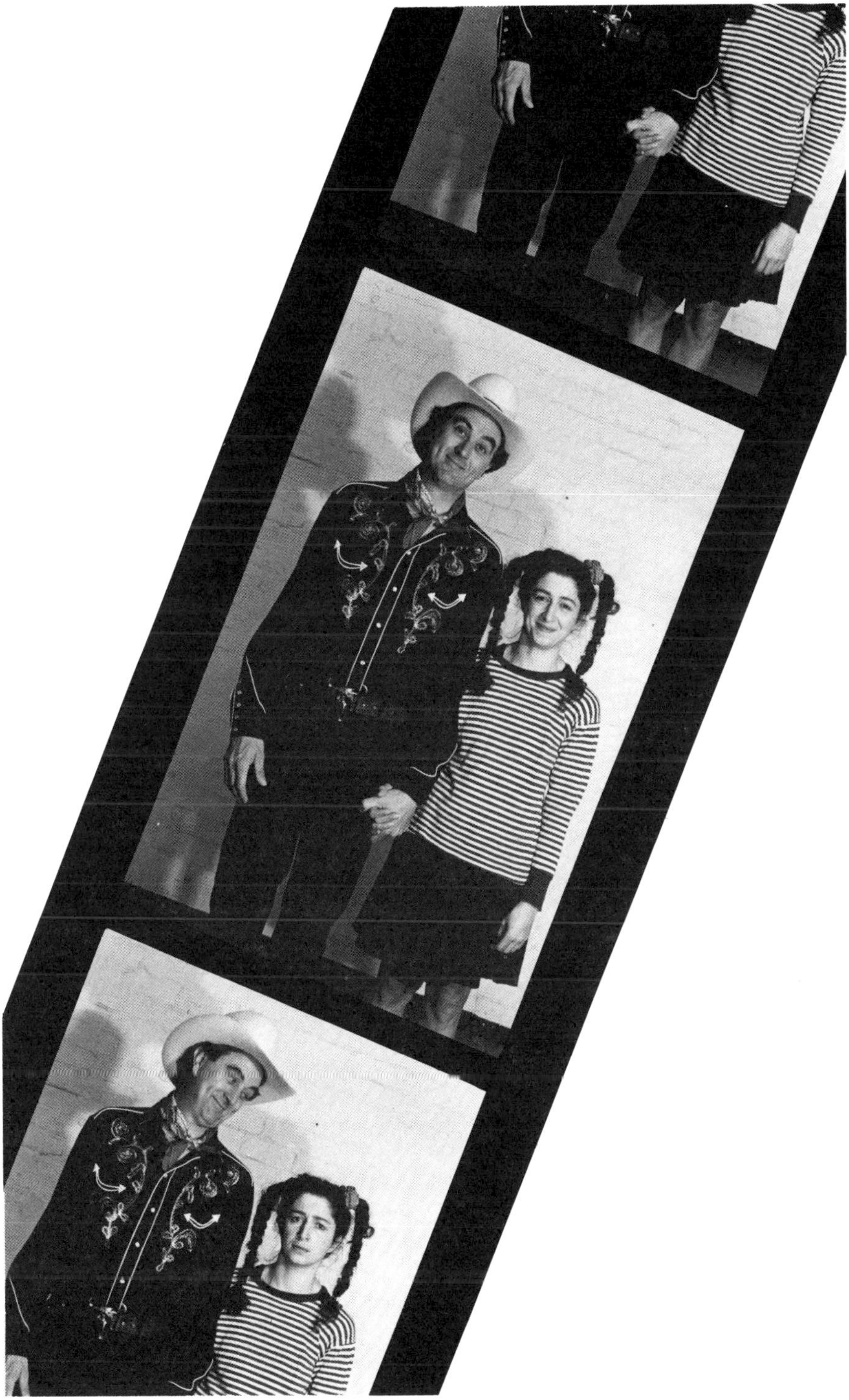

	DARRYN	Yeh, Miss.
	MS DUNNING	Specially knowing how tough things are for you sometimes.
	DARRYN	Me, Miss?
	MS DUNNING	The thing about kindness is, it's catching. Just like cruelty. The more you put out, the more comes back to you. Do you understand what I'm saying Darryn?
	DARRYN	Nuh, Miss.
	MS DUNNING	Well, never mind.
	DARRYN	Alright Miss.
	MS DUNNING	Well, I've got lots of tidying up to do after the barbecue. But Darryn –
	DARRYN	Yeh, Miss?
	MS DUNNING	If you ever need anyone to talk things over with – things that might be making you unhappy, I'll be there – any time. OK?
	DARRYN	Yeh, Miss.

MS DUNNING *exits.* AMANDA *and* MEGAN *enter on either side of* ROWENA *like boxing seconds.* ROWENA *is wrecked. She signs that she can't go through with it.*

	AMANDA	Yes you can. You can do it.
	DARRYN	What's the matter, Batts? Lost your appetite?
	MEGAN	[*to lunch box*] Eat up your nice flies for Darryn, froggy.

ROWENA *decides to make a break for it,* AMANDA *stops her.*

	AMANDA	You're just tense. Jiggle or something. I know, hang over.

AMANDA *shoves* ROWENA *forward and beats her on the back and shakes her arms out of their sockets in a fair imitation of* DAD.

		Now. Breathe deep! [ROWENA *does.*] Again!
	DARRYN	Look Batty, are you gonna race or what?
	AMANDA	[*to* ROWENA] Now. Like I told you I'm faster than him

and you've already beat me.

ROWENA *signs, 'it was the angle of the camera'.*

Nah. You're the fastest, trust me. OK? [*To* DARRYN.] She's ready.

ROWENA *signs, 'no she's not'.*

MEGAN   Good luck Ro!

DARRYN *grabs the lunch box from* MEGAN *and looks inside.*

DARRYN   Just checkin'. [*He returns it.*].

AMANDA   On your marks.

DARRYN   Not you, Cosgrove! Think I'm dumb or somethin'? [TAMMY *is passing.*] You! You start the race.

TAMMY   On your marks...

AMANDA   Don't slow down at the end like you did with me.

ROWENA *and* DARRYN *get on their marks.*

ROWENA   That's funny. I'm gonna eat a frog in five minutes and I don't feel a thing.

TAMMY   Get set...

DARRYN   Frogs taste really nice with cheese sauce.

TAMMY   GO!

DARRYN *runs.* ROWENA *doesn't move.*

ROWENA   But how am I gonna make it stay in the cheese sauce?

AMANDA   Go Rowena! GO!!!

She starts running. TAMMY *exits.*

SONG: LEAPIN' LIZARDS.

MUSICIAN   Leapin' lizards there's a frog in my soup
lookin' at me sideways with it's ole snake eyes.

ROWENA   Move legs, move. Maybe it's a poison toad – I'll have to

MUSICIAN	go to hospital. I hope they've got a stomach pump big enough to suck a frog out. I don't think that I can get it down not unless it comes with shoestring fries.
ROWENA	Come on legs! [DARRYN *remains ahead.*] If only Dad was here, he'd be yelling and jumping up and down and telling me I can do it. Move legs, move. [*She has caught up with* DARRYN, *but he edges ahead again.*] I can't do it Dad, I can't do it without you.
MUSICIAN	Pass the ketchup and the mayonnaise Holy cow I think my time has come. Someone tell me what can I do now 'cos my lunch won't stay inside the bun.
ROWENA	Wait on – what's that across the oval! Someone in a yellow and purple shirt? It's him! He's back! I knew he'd come back. Dad! Here I am Dad!

DAD *is not real – but in* ROWENA's *spaced-out mind. She catches up with* DARRYN *and crosses the line inches ahead of him.*

AMANDA	You won! You won!

AMANDA *is hugging* ROWENA *who is trying to sign. Finally she gets untangled and signs to* AMANDA.

> Where did who go? [ROWENA *signs.*] You saw your Dad? I don't think so.

ROWENA *insists.* MS DUNNING *enters carrying the yellow and purple school banner in front of her. It is made of shiny satin and looks just like one of* DAD's *shirts.* ROWENA *had mistaken her for* DAD.

MS DUNNING	Saw the end of your race from back there. Well run both of you – Ro, are you alright? You don't look well.
AMANDA	She's just a bit tired.

ROWENA *slumps down on the ground, she has lost all interest in revenge.* MEGAN *brings out a napkin from her school bag and flaps it over her arm like a waiter. She brings out a salt shaker and a lunch box.*

MS DUNNING	Come to think of it, you don't look well either, Darryn.
AMANDA	It was a tough race.
MS DUNNING	Is that it? Is that all?
DARRYN	Yeh, Miss. [ROWENA *nods*.].
MS DUNNING	OK. [*She leaves.*]
MEGAN	Well, Darryn Peck. You hungry?

MEGAN *hands* AMANDA *the lunch box.*

DARRYN	Er. I'll eat it later.
AMANDA	Sure you will.
DARRYN	I will, I swear, cross my heart and hope to die.
MEGAN	The deal is loser eats the frog – for lunch!
AMANDA	It's lunch-time, Darryn.
MEGAN	You hold him, I'll feed him.

AMANDA *grabs him. He struggles out of her grip.*

DARRYN	Leave me alone! I'm no chicken! I'll eat it.
AMANDA	OK. Close your eyes.
MEGAN	And open your mouth.

DARRYN *does.* MEGAN *approaches him.*

	Hey what happens if he sicks it up?
AMANDA	Megan, yuk!
MEGAN	No really, will he have to eat it again?

They put something in DARRYN*'s mouth. He can't bring himself to swallow it, his cheeks pop.* MS DUNNING *returns with a bin to clean up the oval.*

MS DUNNING	Darryn Peck! Don't you dare! What have I told you

about blowing bubblegum in school premises!

DARRYN *tries to protest through his full mouth.*

> Out with it! [*She holds the bin out.* DARRYN *shakes his head.*] Now!

DARRYN *swallows.*

MS DUNNING Oh very clever! Your insides will gum up, you know that?

DARRYN *hiccups hugely.*

> Serves you right. By the way, where's your prize Ro? I wondered if you wanted to keep it with the other frogs in the class.

MEGAN *opens a lunch box and shows the frog to* MS DUNNING.

> Mmm, a very healthy specimen. [*She shudders.*]

DARRYN But what... what did I... ?

AMANDA Would you like another frog fritter, Darryn?

AMANDA *opens the first lunch box and takes out an apple fritter.* DARRYN *gapes.* AMANDA *and* MEGAN *lick their index fingers and sign 'one up' on their chests.*

MS DUNNING What's going on?

MEGAN We're practicing sign language Miss. Aren't we, Darryn?

MS DUNNING *looks at* DARRYN. *He is forced to agree.*

VOICE [*from off*] Ms Dunning, Ms Dunning! Mr Fowler said you have to come quick. He said, 'That blessed Rowena Batts' locked herself in the stationery cupboard again!

All look at ROWENA, *puzzled, she takes off.*

SCENE TWENTY ONE

Stationery cupboard. ROWENA *rushes in. She knocks on the door. No answer. She tries to open it, she can't. She whistles as loud as she can. No response. She whistles again as* MR FOWLER, *carrying his crowbar enters followed by* AMANDA *and* MS DUNNING.

MR FOWLER   Well, Rowena, I'm sure that would be very useful if we had a dog in the cupboard, but I suspect it's human! Stand back!

He takes to the door with the crowbar. And skins his knuckles.

Damn! Blast! Come out of there, whoever you are! [*Nothing happens.*] So that's the way you want to play it. Good, good, I've given you fair warning, I'm calling a locksmith! [*He exits.*]

MS DUNNING *picks up the crowbar and has a go.* ROWENA *is signing.*

MS DUNNING   What love? What you say?

AMANDA   Ro knows who it is. She wants to have a try.

MS DUNNING   Who is it Ro?

ROWENA *whistles the first verse of 'Heart Like A Fairground'. She waits, nothing happens. Then, from the cupboard,* DAD *takes up the song.*

DAD   But her heart is a fairground
she fills me with pride
and I know she loves me
'cos I got free tickets
to all of the rides.

The door of the cupboard swings open and DAD *steps out. He is wearing the straightest, worstest-fitting suit imaginable.* ROWENA *flings herself into his arms. He looks at* MS DUNNING.

MS DUNNING	You look ridiculous.
DAD	That's what happens when you buy your clothes from a cheese-brain. Bugger doesn't have anything in your size!
AMANDA	My dad sold you a suit?
MS DUNNING	Well, he refused to actually. So I just bunged some money across the counter and took one! Sort him out later.

MR COSGROVE *enters, followed by* MRS COSGROVE.

MR COSGROVE	Oh will you indeed! I demand you return my property forthwith! Call the police someone! This man's a thief!
DAD	Who you calling a thief, mate?
MR COSGROVE	He's threatening me again. You all heard him. I'll have him arrested!
AMANDA	Dad, I don't want you to take this the wrong way, and if I say something to you, you won't leave or anything, will you?
MR COSGROVE	Responsible people don't up and leave! Oh, no, they leave that to hoons and criminals!
AMANDA	That's good, 'cos I really love you and need you but you have to... you have to... p... pull...

AMANDA *turns to* ROWENA *in despair.* ROWENA *signs it.* AMANDA *signs it at her father.*

MR COSGROVE	What are you... ? What is she saying!
MRS COSGROVE	Let's go home Douglas.

She pushes him off.

MR COSGROVE	But what? What did she say? I won't have it — all this secret society stuff. What did she... [*They're gone.*]
AMANDA	He'll calm down in a few days. I'll take that suit back to the shop and change it for a bigger size if you like, Mr Batts.

ROWENA *signs: 'no way!' She rummages in her schoolbag and brings out a package and hands it to* DAD *who reads the back of it.*

DAD   From the mail order mob?

ROWENA *nods. She urges him to open it. Inside is a new satin shirt.* DAD *gazes on its pink glory with longing.*

No...

ROWENA *stamps her foot and nods 'yes'. She tugs his jacket off.*

You sure?

ROWENA *nods.* DAD *changes shirts. The new one has a big black guitar on the back.* DAD *looks into* MS DUNNING*'s eyes. She floats towards him gazing back into his. She drops the crowbar on his foot.*

The whole company assembles. They sing and sign the following version of 'Blabbermouth'

My baby is the sweetest little thing
That I ever dreamed of
Her hair is just like silken fronds
that wind around my heart
Her hands are like two hot mince pies
But when I look into her eyes
I swear that I will never part

Chorus:
She's the biggest ever blabbermouth
Her lips reach right from north to south
Her voice is like the thunder
That makes rain fall from the skies
She's my blabber blabbermouth
Her lips reach right from north to south
And I'm a gonna love that gal until the day I die.

Her skin is like a satin pillow
I could lay and dream on

She has the cutest little
Mole upon her cheek
She has a long and scraggy neck
But I'm in love so what the heck
I'm gonna see my baby every evening of the week

Repeat chorus.
Her face is like the sun that brings
Out the little flowers
Her eyes are little moon-beams
That peep out between the rain
Her figure's like a mountain-side
On which a herd of goats has died
But when I'm with my baby
I don't ever feel no pain.

Repeat chorus.

THE END

MORE TEENAGE PLAYS FROM CURRENCY

FOSSILS
Manuel Aston

Homo-parentithicus. Found in most urban parts of Australia. Usually roams in pairs. Over-protective toward off-spring. Parents!! In the tradition of *Dags* by Debra Oswald and *Boss of the Pool* by Mary Morris, *Fossils* takes a look at the relationship between parents and teenagers.
ISBN 0 86819 399 2

WHAT IS THE MATTER WITH MARY JANE?
Wendy Harmer

A powerful and urgent message about the traumas of the eating disorders anorexia nervosa and bulimia, told with humour, warmth and great understanding. Published with a full study guide.
ISBN 0 86819 480 8

A PROPERTY OF THE CLAN
Nick Enright

When a young girl is murdered at the hands of one of her male contemporaries, what is the aftermath? How will her friends cope with the shock of such a tragedy? Is an understanding of violence ever possible? Written for the Freewheels TIE Theatre Co, the play deals with these issues with honesty, sensitivity and intelligence.
ISBN 0 86819 360 7

LOCKIE LEONARD, HUMAN TORPEDO
Paige Gibbs, adapted from the novel by Tim Winton

Lockie Leonard, human torpedo, has arrived in town... He gives the teachers a hard time, and surfs like there's no tomorrow - but no one wants to know the city boy whose Dad's a cop and doesn't believe in violence. Then Lockie becomes the president of the new surfers' club and the boyfriend of the most popular girl in school.
ISBN 0 86819 478 6

BACKSTAGE PASS
Wendy Harmer

Rock fans Janis and Razz are waiting anxiously for a glimpse of their rock idol, Stax Jackson, although Razz's brother Gator is more interested in his skateboard. Stax is really gorgeous - or is he? And who is Brian Cronk? Cannon-the-roadie reveals some very interesting information.
ISBN 0 86819 311 9

GROMMITTS
Kathy Lette

In her inimitable language, Kathy Lette, author of *Puberty Blues* and *Girls' Night Out*, helps her characters sort out their multicultural and personal differences, and similarities, where being a Waxhead, Westie, Headbanger or Grommitt can mean the difference between life and death!!
ISBN 0 86819 200 7

SPITTING CHIPS
Peta Murray

Sybil, *aka*, Spud, lives with her father who won't discuss Sybil's dead mother. Her reluctant friendship with an old woman helps both of them address their loneliness and deal with the future. Peta Murray is the award-winning author of the very popular *Wallflowering*.
ISBN 0 86819 406 9

Available from good bookshops and Book Suppliers.

Currency Press

PO Box 452,

Paddington, NSW 2021